Quiet Wyatt

Written by Larry Dane Brimner
Illustrated by Rusty Fletcher

Children's Press®
A Division of Scholastic Inc.
New York • Toronto • London • Auckland • Sydney
Mexico City • New Delhi • Hong Kong
Danbury, Connecticut

For Carson and Cassidy Brimner.
—L. D. B.

For my boys, Will and Sam, who are seldom quiet,
but are always the best part of my day.
—R. F.

Reading Consultant

Cecilia Minden-Cupp, PhD
Former Director of the Language and Literacy Program
Harvard Graduate School of Education
Cambridge, Massachusetts

Cover design: The Design Lab
Interior design: Herman Adler

Library of Congress Cataloging-in-Publication Data

Brimner, Larry Dane.
 Quiet Wyatt / by Larry Dane Brimner; illustrated by Rusty Fletcher;
reading consultant, Cecilia Minden-Cupp.
      p. cm. — (A rookie reader—opposites)
   ISBN-13: 978-0-531-17543-9 (lib. bdg.)   978-0-531-17777-8 (pbk.)
   ISBN-10: 0-531-17543-X (lib. bdg.)   0-531-17777-7 (pbk.)
  1. English language—Synonyms and antonyms—Juvenile literature.
I. Fletcher, Rusty. II. Title. III. Series.
  PE1591.B74 2007
  428.1—dc22   2006027034

CHILDREN'S PRESS, and A ROOKIE READER®, and associated logos
are trademarks and/or registered trademarks of Scholastic Library
Publishing. SCHOLASTIC and associated logos are trademarks and/or
registered trademarks of Scholastic Inc.
1 2 3 4 5 6 7 8 9 10 R 16 15 14 13 12 11 10 09 08 07

In a loud, loud town
is a loud, loud street.

On this loud, loud street
there is a loud, loud school.

And in this loud, loud school
stands quiet, quiet Wyatt.

Why is Wyatt so, so quiet?
Can he roar like a lion?

9

He can roar like a lion.
But today he's quiet like a mouse.

Can he howl under the moon?

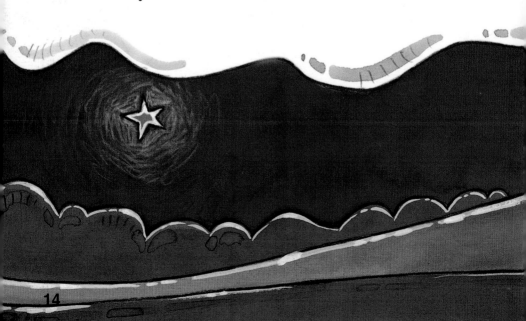

He can howl under the moon.
But today he's as silent as the stars.

Can he rumble like thunder?

He can rumble like thunder.
But today he sounds as soft as
one tiny raindrop.

Listen to Wyatt roar like a lion!

Hear him howl under the moon.

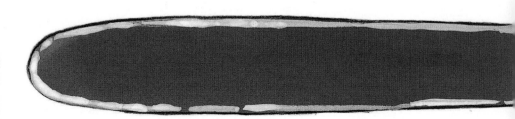

Cover your ears when he rumbles like thunder!

But not today.

Usually there's no one louder than Wyatt.

But sometimes it's good to be quiet!

Word List (58 words)

(Words in **bold** are used as opposites.)

a	him	no	**soft**	thunder
and	**howl**	not	sometimes	tiny
as	in	on	sounds	to
be	is	one	stands	today
but	it's	**quiet**	stars	town
can	like	raindrop	street	under
cover	lion	**roar**	than	usually
ears	listen	rumble	the	when
good	**loud**	rumbles	there	why
he	louder	school	there's	Wyatt
hear	moon	**silent**	this	your
he's	mouse	so		

About the Author

Quiet Larry Dane Brimner is the author of many titles in the Rookie Reader series, among them *Here Comes Trouble*, *Raindrops*, and *Cats!* He is also the author of *The Littlest Wolf* and *Subways: The Story of Tunnels, Tubes, and Tracks*.

About the Illustrator

Rusty Fletcher works from his home studio in the historic village of Granville, Ohio. Rusty feels lucky to be able to do what he really loves—create artwork for children's books. He has two boys of his own, Will and Sam, who are sometimes quiet and sometimes very, VERY loud.